SUPER SCIENCE
MAGIC

SUPER SCIENCE
MAGIC

by Sandra Markle
Illustrated by Jamie Smith

SCHOLASTIC INC.

New York   Toronto   London   Auckland   Sydney
Mexico City   New Delhi   Hong Kong   Buenos Aires

ISBN 0-439-28136-9

12 11 10 9 8 7 6 5 4 3 2 1   1 2 3 4 5 6/0
                                                      40
Printed in the U.S.A.
First Scholastic printing, September 2001

For the students at Hillview Christian School in
Christchurch, New Zealand.

The author would like to thank Dr. Gerald Krockover, Professor of
Earth Atmospheric Science Curriculum and Instruction at Purdue
University, for sharing his enthusiasm and expertise. The author
would also like to thank Skip Jeffery for his help building, testing,
and researching, but especially for sharing the fun of performing
science magic.

Contents

It's Show Time!

You can become a magician and put on a terrific show — with a little help from science. In this book, you'll discover how to use basic science concepts to make a ball float in midair, change glue into rubbery plastic, blow up a balloon without touching it, make an invisible message appear, and lots more.

Here are some tips to help you put on a successful show.

- Always try out your science magic tricks before you perform them for an audience.

- Take time to get ready for your performance. Collect all the supplies you'll need and group them together for each science magic trick. You may need to use a chemical, such as vinegar, more than once. In that case, pour what you'll need into separate containers — one for each stunt. You'll need water for some stunts, so fill a plastic container, such as a milk jug.

- Set the groups of supplies on a table in the order you'll need to use them. Or put the supplies for each trick on separate trays. Number the trays and have a helper deliver them to you in the correct order. If you don't have trays, use boxes with the top flaps cut off.

- Prepare all the "Get Ready" activities before show time.

- Work carefully, following the activity instructions. Have an adult partner help you use tools, such as knives.

- Act the part of a science magician. Choose a name for yourself, such as "The Wiz." Be sure to get an adult's permission and then transform an old white T-shirt into a costume with textile markers. As you perform, wave your hands in the air and say magic-sounding words, such as "Abracadabra science!"

- Have fun.

  Now, on with the show!

Gee-wizard Tricks!

Sometimes when two different kinds of chemicals are mixed together a reaction happens. The chemicals may change color. They may even produce a completely new compound. Here are some chemical reactions you can use to amaze your audience.

1. Presto Pennies

You can make dirty pennies become shiny clean as quick as one-two-three.

You'll Need

- **6 dark-colored pennies**
- **Sturdy paper plate**
- **1 teaspoon salt**
- **2 tablespoons vinegar**

Perform

Arrange the pennies at the center of the paper plate. Make sure that none of the pennies touch or overlap. Sprinkle the salt on the pennies and then pour the vinegar on top of the salt. Wave your hand over the pennies and say "Abracadabra science!" The pennies will look like shiny, bright copper.

Behind the Magic

You can understand why this trick works once you know a secret about the pennies. They weren't dark because they were dirty. They were tarnished. What looks like dirt is really a chemical that forms on the surface of copper when it comes in contact with oxygen, one of the gases in the air.

Vinegar is a kind of chemical called an acid. Acids that you can eat, like vinegar and lemon juice, taste sour. Acids also often react with metals. The vinegar dissolved the coating on the pennies, exposing the clean copper underneath. The reaction would have happened even without the salt, but the salt sped up the reaction. So the shiny copper appeared quickly — as if by magic.

Magic in Action

Plumbers polish tarnished copper pipes but not just to make them shiny. They remove tarnish so they can use melted metal to make pieces of pipe stick together. The melted metal sticks best to untarnished copper. By joining pieces of pipe, plumbers create a system water can flow through in homes, offices, and factories.

2. Make Invisible Messages Appear

You already discovered some magic you can do with chemicals called acids. There is also another set of special chemicals, called bases. When acids and bases mix, there's usually a reaction. Here's one that looks like magic!

You'll Need

1 tablespoon baking soda (a base)

1 tablespoon water

Paper cup

Cotton swab

Plain white paper

1/4 cup purple grape juice (an acid) (Read the package label to make sure you use 100 percent grape juice rather than a grape-flavored drink.)

Small mixing bowl

Paper towel

Getting Ready

While you're setting up, mix up some *invisible* ink. Mix a solution that's half baking soda and half water. For example, dissolve one tablespoon of baking soda in one tablespoon of water in the paper cup. Dip a cotton swab into the liquid and paint a message, such as "Hi," on a sheet of plain white paper. Then let the paper dry completely.

Perform

When you're ready to make the word appear, pour grape juice into the mixing bowl and wad up the paper towel. Dip the bottom edge of the towel into the juice and dab it onto the paper. Start at the top and move quickly down the paper. The secret word will become visible when touched by the grape juice.

Behind the Magic

When your message dried, some particles of baking soda were deposited on the paper. When the grape juice, an acid, came in contact with the baking soda, a base, a reaction happened. This caused the white baking soda to turn gray, making the invisible message readable.

3. Kaboom-a-balloon

You can create more magic with another acid-base reaction — inflate a balloon without blowing into it. This is the same science magic used to inflate car air bags and protect passengers.

You'll Need

Scissors

Paper towel

2 tablespoons baking soda

1-liter plastic soda bottle

1/4 cup vinegar

Balloon

Perform

Cut off one-fourth of the paper towel. Put two tablespoons of baking soda on this small piece of towel and roll it into a tube. Twist the ends shut to

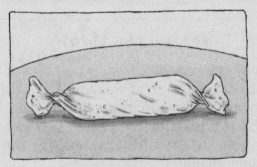

seal. Push this packet into the bottle. Pour in the vinegar. Slide the neck of the balloon over the

mouth of the bottle. Gently rock the bottle from side to side to help the vinegar soak into the paper towel packet. Within seconds, the balloon will inflate, but don't expect it to swell as fully as it would if you blew into it.

Behind the Magic

The bottle was already full of air when you started. When the vinegar and baking soda mixed inside the bottle, the chemical reaction gave off bubbles of carbon dioxide gas — the same waste gas you breathe out. Like a glass overflowing with water, some of the air and gas spilled out of the bottle, inflating the balloon.

Magic in Action

Car air bags are cloth bags that inflate very quickly — in less than one-twentieth of a second. The reaction starts when an impact triggers a sensor. That sensor turns on a switch, sending electricity to a heating element, which heats up two chemicals, causing them to react and give off nitrogen gas. *Whoosh!* The bag inflates. Then, because the bag is full of holes, it starts to deflate immediately. To see why this is important, blow up a balloon and hold the neck pinched shut. Push the sealed balloon against the wall. Then push again while letting the air escape from the balloon. The deflating bag acts as a better cushion against a sudden impact.

Small children can get hurt when they're suddenly struck by an inflating air bag. So now automakers are working on finding ways to make air bags safer. One idea being tested puts sensors in the seat. Then the air bag checks the passenger's weight and only switches on for passengers above a set weight.

4. Whip Up Plastic

Amaze your friends by changing glue into plastic!

You'll Need

1/2 cup water

2 paper cups

1 tablespoon borax* (It's inexpensive and found in the laundry area of most local supermarkets.)

1/4 cup white glue

Plastic spoon

Bowl of water

*Handle the borax only with a spoon. When you are finished performing, throw the plastic spoon and paper cups away.

Perform

Pour the water into one of the paper cups. Add the borax and stir until most of the crystals dissolve. When this happens, the molecules of borax become suspended in the water.

Pour the white glue into the other paper cup. Then pour in the borax liquid. Say "Abracadabra science!" and stir the glue with the spoon until it becomes a white glob. Use the spoon to press out any bubbles of liquid glue. Transfer the white glob to the bowl of water and squeeze until no more liquid glue oozes out. There you have it — plastic!

Behind the Magic

To understand how this trick works, you need to know something about the structure of plastic. Like all matter, it's made up of building blocks called molecules. Molecules of plastic, though, are linked together, forming long chains.

Magic in Action

The very first plastics, such as tar, shellac, and tree sap, occurred naturally. In the 1800s, American Wesley Hyatt figured out a way to create a strong plastic out of plant material. This first artificial plastic was called celluloid (say SELL-u-loyd). Hyatt used it to produce billiard balls, combs, and other items that were usually made of ivory. The celluloid items were as strong as the ivory ones, but they had a serious fault. If struck, they easily exploded. After a lot of testing, Hyatt discovered that adding camphor from laurel trees to the plastic solved this problem.

A number of years later, American Leo Baekeland found a way to combine two chemicals to make an even more useful plastic. This material wouldn't melt and didn't dissolve in most chemicals. It was also very lightweight. Called Bakelite™, it was used to produce many different products, such as radios and jewelry.

5. Now You See It — Now You Don't!

You can make Styrofoam™ peanuts magically disappear.

You'll Need

Nail polish remover that contains acetone (Check the label.)

Glass jar with a wide mouth

Bag of Styrofoam peanuts (Test to be sure the peanuts are Styrofoam by dropping one in a glass of water to see if it dissolves. If it doesn't dissolve, it's Styrofoam.)

Getting Ready

Before the performance begins, pour enough nail polish remover into the jar to cover the bottom.

Perform

Start by choosing a member of the audience to help you. Tell your helper to fill the jar with the Styrofoam peanuts. Then ask to check his or her work. Pick up the jar and wiggle it to swirl the liquid. The peanuts will suddenly shrink and disappear. Exclaim, "Oh, my!" Then ask your helper to please try again. Repeat this process several times before announcing you've just played a science magic trick on your helper. Share what happened.

Behind the Magic

Styrofoam is made up of long chains of molecules. The acetone causes the chemical links that bind these molecules together to break. Because it's possible to break apart long molecular chains, some plastics can be recycled. That's lucky, because in the United States alone, 75 billion pounds (34 billion kg) of plastics are produced each year.

Magic in Action

Paintbrushes, park benches, carpets, and lots of other useful products can be made from four kinds of plastics — those labeled V, PS, PP, and PETE. Recycled plastics are also being turned into building products that can be used in place of wood.

Eye Tricks

These tricks are possible because your eyes and brain must work together to let you see. While the brain interprets signals from the eyes very quickly, this process doesn't happen instantly.

6. See a Ghost!

Create this illusion to prove seeing isn't always believing. It's the same magic that makes cartoon characters appear to come to life.

You'll Need

- **Glass or cup**
- **Poster board**
- **Pencil**
- **Scissors**
- **Colored markers**
- **Hole punch**
- **Two 18-inch-long pieces of string**

Get Ready

You'll need to make the following prop to get ready to perform this trick. First, set the glass or cup upside down on the poster board and trace a circle around the outside of the glass or cup. Cut out this disk. Use the markers to draw a fish on

 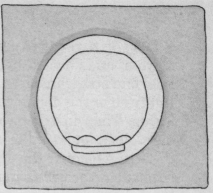

FRONT   **BACK**

the center of the disk. Then turn the disk over and draw an upside-down fishbowl. Make the fishbowl fill the disk.

Next, punch a hole in the center on either side of the disk. Tie the ends of one string together. Thread the string through one hole just far enough to form a loop. Thread the other end of the string through this loop and pull it tight. Repeat, looping the other string through the other hole.

Note: You may want to prepare enough disks for each member of your audience to share the science magic.

Perform

When you're ready to perform, choose one member of your audience to help you. Have that person hold one string in each hand — pulling the string tight. Turn the disk over and over to wind up the string. Then instruct your helper to stare at the disk. Next, let go of the disk, allowing the unwinding string to make the disk spin. Ask your helper to report how the fish changed. Your helper should see the fish suddenly appear to be inside the fishbowl.

Behind the Magic

This illusion is possible because the brain is still processing the fish image when it receives signals for the fishbowl's image. The brain also starts processing that image, interpreting the two images as one.

You could make disks with different image pairs, such as a face and a window or a bird and a nest. Remember, though, when something has a definite top and bottom, like a bird or a nest, the image on the back of the disk must be drawn upside down. Then as the disk spins, it will appear to be right side up.

7. The Amazing Floating Finger

Guide your audience through this neat trick.

You'll Need

Your hands
Your eyes

Perform

Tell the audience to hold up their two index fingers. Have them turn their hands so their index fingers touch. Next, have them touch the joined fingertips to their nose.

Instruct your audience to look at something in

the distance over the top of their fingers. Then have them slowly push their joined index fingers away from their noses. Tell your audience to keep staring at the same distant point during this process. As soon as their fingers are about a hand's-length away from their noses, they'll see a surprise. Instead of seeing two joined fingers, they will see a piece of a finger floating between two fingertips.

Behind the Magic

Special muscles change the shape of the eyes' lenses as focus is shifted from close to faraway objects. Usually, the brain receives just one set of signals at a time to analyze — either a close-up or a distant view. This illusion appears because the eye is sending two separate sets of signals to the brain at the same time — those for the close-up image and those for the distant view.

Wet and Wild Stunts

Like all matter, water is made up of tiny things called molecules. Water molecules have a special trait — they tend to cling together like two pieces of sticky tape. You can take advantage of this to perform experiments that appear totally amazing!

8. The Ring Trick

Announce that you will make a ring of toothpicks shrink and expand without touching it. Then have your audience gather around a pan full of water to watch the action.

You'll Need

Pie or cake pan

Water

6 flat wooden toothpicks

Liquid dishwashing soap

Perform

Fill the pan nearly full of water. Dip the tip of one toothpick into the liquid soap. Set it aside. Lay the five remaining toothpicks one at a time on the surface of the water. Arrange the five toothpicks in a ring formation, overlapping the tips.

Now in front of your audience, pick up the soapy toothpick. Say something magical and touch the soapy end of the toothpick to the center of the ring. The toothpicks will zip apart.

Behind the Magic

Because water molecules naturally cling together, the water's surface acts as if it has an invisible layer stretched across it. This layer is called water's *surface tension*. The toothpicks floated on this layer. Soap molecules break apart the bonds that cause water molecules to cling together. This effect spreads outward in all directions. As this happens, the surface tension is greater in front of the toothpicks, so they are pulled to where the surface tension is strongest.

9. Magic Racing Fish

Now, while your audience remains gathered around, use what you discovered about water's surface tension to perform another stunt. Send plastic fish racing through the water!

You'll Need

Colored plastic report cover

Scissors

Rectangular cake pan

Water

3 toothpicks

Liquid dishwashing soap

Permanent marker

Getting Ready

First, cut out three plastic fish about 2 inches (5 cm) long from the plastic report cover. Snip a V shape in the center of the tail. Use the marking pen to number the fish 1, 2, and 3. Fill the cake pan

nearly full of water. Dip the tips of the three tooth-picks into the liquid soap and set these aside.

Perform

Pick three helpers — one to launch each of the fish. Present each helper with a soap-dipped toothpick. Announce that the winner will be the fish that travels farthest. Call on your audience to vote with a show of hands on whether they believe fish 1, fish 2, or fish 3 will win.

Float the fish in a line with their tails at one end of the pan. Instruct your helpers, on your signal, to touch the soapy tip of the toothpick to the water in the center of their fish's tail. Then count down to launch the race. The fish will go zipping toward the opposite side of the pan.

Behind the Magic

The plastic fish float on the water's shrinking surface tension. The soap at the fish's tail breaks the surface tension. As this effect spreads, the fish are tugged forward, riding the shrinking surface tension toward the edge of the pan. To make your fish race again, you will need to rinse the fish and the pan. Then refill the pan. Can you figure out why you'll need to do this?

10. The Stalk Caper

You can use the fact that water molecules tend to cling together to perform more magic — make green celery leaves turn red!

You'll Need

Bud vase

Water

Red food coloring

2 celery stalks with leaves

Scissors

Cardboard box

Getting Ready

Fill the bud vase half full with water. Drip in enough food coloring to turn the water bright red. Trim off the bottom end of the celery stalk and place it in the water. Do this about an hour before show time. Set it inside a box that's big enough to hide it completely.

Perform

Repeat setting up the trick as part of your performance. After you have set it up, say "Abracadabra science!" Set the new celery stalk inside the box and whisk out the one you prepared earlier. Now you can display the results — a stalk with red-streaked leaves.

Behind the Magic

Snip the celery stalk lengthwise to discover the red streaks inside. These streaks are really long tubes formed by a stack of cells. In the living plant, these tubes carried water and minerals up from the roots to the leaves. In this science magic trick, the tubes carried the red coloring up to the leaves.

To see how the water moved cell by cell up through these tubes, try this. Touch the edge of a paper towel to the red-colored water. The edge of the paper will turn red as the water moves into the spaces between the paper fibers. Because water molecules cling together, the water in the paper pulls along more water. The water molecules already trapped in the paper are then pushed up into higher empty spaces. The process is repeated and a column of red-colored water climbs up the paper.

11. Blooming Magic

Here's another version of the celery stalk trick you can perform. The result this time will make a white carnation turn half red and half blue.

You'll Need

2 glasses

Water

Red and blue food coloring

Safety knife*

2 white carnations (You'll find these in your local supermarket's floral section or in a florist shop.)

Cardboard box

*Have an adult partner help you slice the flower's stem.

Getting Ready

On the day before your performance, fill two glasses with water. Add red food coloring to one and blue food coloring to the other. Have an adult split one flower's stem about halfway up.

Perform

Set the glasses side by side and carefully place one half of the flower's stem in each glass. Let the flower sit overnight.

On the day of the performance, place the carnation with the split stem into the cardboard box. When it's time to perform this trick, announce that you can make the flower change color. Hold up the white carnation, wave it in the air, and then whip it into the box. Drop that flower and pick up the other one, being careful to hold the split stem together. This carnation will be half blue and half red. Finish by placing the colored carnation in the vase and presenting it to your parent or a member of the audience.

Behind the Magic

Like the celery, long tubes in the carnation's stem carry water and nutrients to the bloom. The water carries the food coloring and deposits it in the flower's petals.

12. Solve a Mystery

Impress your audience by naming which of three inks was used to write a message.

You'll Need

Masking tape

Scissors

3 different types of black watercolor markers*

4 coffee filters

Tape

4 pencils

4 tall glasses (or three 1-liter, clear plastic bottles with the tops cut off)

Water

Cardboard box

You will also need a partner when you perform this trick.

*Check to be sure the markers are watercolor, not permanent ink. Only watercolor ink will separate in water.

Getting Ready

On the day before your science magic show, use the following investigation steps to discover something about the three different black inks. First, cut three pieces of masking tape and place one piece on each

40

of the three black markers. Label them 1, 2, and 3. Cut three identical strips — about 2 by 6 inches (5 by 15 cm) — from the coffee filters. Put tape at the top of each strip and label these 1, 2, and 3. Tape the labeled end of each strip to a pencil. Use marker 1 to make an ink dot about the size of the tip of your little finger halfway up strip 1. Do the same with each of the other two markers. Pour water into each glass so it will be just deep enough to reach the bottom of the strip. Place one paper strip in each glass, resting the pencil on the rim. Then

watch what happens! The water will appear to climb up the paper strip, changing the ink spot into a flame-shaped pattern of colors. Remove the sample strips from the pencils, let them dry, and keep them hidden on the day of the performance.

Perform

When you're ready to perform this science magic

stunt, have your adult partner use one of the numbered black markers to write a word on a coffee filter. Turn your back so you don't see which ink is used. Have your partner display the number on the marker to the audience before placing it back in the set.

Next, cut a strip out of the word, tape it to a pencil, and place the strip in the glass. Add enough water to cover the bottom of the filter. Walk around, displaying the glass and filter to the audience while the water rises through the paper. As soon as the flame of color appears, compare it to the samples. Then identify the mystery marker.

Behind the Magic

If you look closely at the coffee filter with a magnifying glass, you'll see tiny spaces between the fibers. The water flows into these spaces. Because water molecules tend to cling together, more will be pulled along. Repeating this process, the water will appear to slowly climb the paper strip. The colored dyes in the ink dissolve in water, meaning the bits of coloring matter become suspended in the water. Different dyes have different densities. So those that are denser — or heavier — are deposited on the paper fibers first, while less dense ones are carried farther. The colorful flame shape reveals which dyes were combined to create the ink. Comparing the flame pattern produced by the mystery ink to the samples reveals which marker was used.

Magic in Action

Forensic scientists, investigators who use science to solve crimes, use the same magic you just performed. They may want to identify the ink used to write a letter. Or they may want to discover if part of a will or other document was changed. Every kind of ink — even every batch of ink — is slightly different.

13. Make an Exploding Rainbow

Oil and milk don't mix. Use this fact to delight your audience.

You'll Need

Pie pan

Whole milk

Red, blue, green, and yellow food coloring

Liquid dishwashing soap

Perform

Fill the pie pan nearly full of whole milk. Have your audience gather around the pie pan. Drip in three drops of each of these food colors: red, blue, green, and yellow. Say something magical and then pour in the liquid dishwashing soap. Your audience will be amazed at what happens next! The colors will appear to explode. You probably won't want to wait, but this kaleidoscopic display may continue for as long as twenty minutes.

Behind the Magic

Milk appears to be just a white liquid, but it's really tiny drops of fat suspended in a watery liquid. The dishwashing soap breaks the surface tension of the milk and interacts with both the watery liquid and the fat. One end of each soap molecule attaches to a fat molecule, while the other attaches to a water molecule. This reaction creates currents that swirl and mix the drops of food coloring.

14. Dancing Drops

Some liquids are denser than others. You can use this fact to create an illusion that looks like magic.

You'll Need

A tall, clear water glass
Water
Vegetable oil
Salt

Perform

Fill the glass about two-thirds full with water. Pour in enough oil to form a layer about an inch (2.5 cm) deep. The oil is less dense, and so it will float on top of the water.

Next, shake on some salt, spreading a layer across the surface of the oil. Command the oil to dance. Hold the glass up so your audience can see the magical dancing drops in action. To keep the oil drops dancing, add more salt.

Behind the Magic

The solid salt grains are denser than the water. So the salt sinks through the oil, carrying drops of oil down with it. Salt dissolves in water, though. When the salt grains dissolve, the oil drops are released and float up again.

Magic in Action

In 1964, Englishman Craven Walker used the fact
that different liquids have different densities to
create a special light — the Lava Lite™. A Lava
Lite is a tall, thin glass full of liquid, with a layer of
colored wax on the bottom. A light in the base heats
up this wax, softening it. Drops of liquid wax are
less dense than water, and so they float up to the
surface. There the drops cool, becoming solid wax
again. The solid wax is denser than the water and
sinks back to the bottom. Then the process begins
all over again.

15. Make a Blizzard Bottle!

Some liquids are denser than others. You can use this science fact to create something magical.

You'll Need

A small plastic bottle, such as a water bottle, with a screw-on lid

Rubbing alcohol (It's found in most supermarkets and drugstores. Read the label to be sure it's isopropyl alcohol.)

Food coloring

Clear vegetable oil

A small jar of glitter

Sequins or other small, colorful items, such as little buttons

Duct tape

Getting Ready

Before show time, remove any label on the outside of the bottle. Be sure the decorative items you plan to add will fit easily through the bottle's neck.

Perform

Start this stunt by filling the bottle one-fourth full with rubbing alcohol. Add a couple of drops of food coloring. Slowly pour in the vegetable oil until the bottle is full to within an inch (2.5 cm) of the top. The oil is denser than the alcohol, so it will sink. Walk around, displaying the bottle while this is happening.

Next, pour in as much glitter as you like and drop in the colorful items. Pour in enough oil to fill the bottle to the rim. Screw the lid on tightly. Seal with the duct tape.

Turn the bottle upside down to start the blizzard effect.

Behind the Magic

As the bottle is tipped, the alcohol is briefly mixed with the oil. Then the two liquids quickly separate. Bubbles form as the less dense alcohol rises to the top of the oil again. Any decorative items denser than the oil will settle to the bottom. Any items less dense than the alcohol will float to the top.

16. Make Them Mix!

Now demonstrate for your audience how you can make two liquids that usually don't mix blend together and stay mixed.

You'll Need

1 egg

Cup

Fork

Clear plastic wrap

Bowl

Ice cubes

Self-sealing plastic bag

1 cup salad oil

Pint-sized clear plastic container with
    large mouth

2 tablespoons lemon juice

Getting Ready

To set up for your performance, crack an egg into a cup. Whip the egg with a fork. Cover the cup with the plastic wrap and set the cup in a bowl that is half filled with ice.

Perform

Pour the salad oil into the pint-sized container.

Slowly pour in the lemon juice. Hold up the container, pointing out that the oil floats up to the top of the lemon juice. Explain that the two liquids are different densities and usually don't mix. Then announce that you can make these two liquids mix. Pour the egg into the glass. Say "Abracadabra science!" while you stir the liquids with the fork. The result is a creamy mixture.

Behind the Magic

The egg coated the droplets of oil and lemon juice, trapping them suspended together. When droplets of one kind of matter are suspended in another, the result is called an emulsion. This creamy emulsion is one you may have eaten on a sandwich or salad — mayonnaise.

Creepy Air Tricks

Air is the perfect substance for performing magic. It's invisible, but if you've ever blown up a balloon, you know it takes up space. Air can also exert pressure, and moving air can do things that will amaze you.

17. Make Water Float in Midair

With a little help from science, you can keep water from spilling out of a glass when you turn it upside down.

You'll Need

Paper towels — the super-soaker-upper kind
1 sturdy plastic picnic plate
A small glass, such as a juice glass
Water
Red food coloring

Getting Ready

Fold the paper towel in fourths and place it on the plate. Fill the glass nearly full of water and add red food coloring.

Perform

When you're ready to perform this science magic stunt, put the towel on the plate. Hold the towel in place as you turn the plate upside down over the glass. Use one hand to hold the glass and the other to hold the plate. Lift the glass and plate and turn them upside down. Be sure to keep the glass straight.

Say "Abracadabra science!" and continue to hold on to the glass while letting go of the plate. The plate will stay in place, trapping the water inside the glass. Of course, you will want to practice this stunt a number of times before trying it with your partner.

Behind the Magic

The water's surface tension helps hold the water together where it's in contact with the plate. As the plate begins to separate slightly from the glass, water begins to flow out. This creates an area of lower pressure above the water inside the glass. Then the forces pressing down and the force of the air pressure below the plate pushing up are balanced. The plate is held against the bottom of the glass. It's important to keep the glass straight, because tipping it lets air slip inside, undoing the balance. Then the water rushes out with a big splash!

18. Float a Head

Now use the power of fast-moving air to perform another magic trick — make a ghostly head hover in midair.

You'll Need

Permanent marker

Ping-Pong ball (These come in different weights — the lighter the weight of the ball, the higher it will float.)

Blow-dryer

Getting Ready

Use the marker to draw a face on the Ping-Pong ball.

Perform

To start the ghostly head floating, switch the blow-dryer on "high." Aim its jet of air straight up. Then release the ball into this fast-flowing column of air.

Behind the Magic

You already discovered that air has pressure. A fast-moving jet of air, though, exerts less pressure than the slow-moving air around it. So the Ping-Pong ball is trapped in the fast-moving column of air.

19. More Air Tricks

Here are two more ways to amaze your audience, using the fact that fast-moving air has less pressure.

1. Make a paper strip float up.

To perform this trick, you'll need a strip of notebook paper about 2 inches (5 cm) wide. Ask your audience to vote with a show of hands on whether they think blowing on the strip of paper will make it sink or rise. Then demonstrate what happens. Hold either side of one end of the strip between your fingers. Place this end just below your lower lip. Then blow — hard. Your fast-flowing breath moving across the top of the paper strip will have less pressure than the slow-moving air underneath. The strip will float up.

2. Make two pieces of paper move together.
This time, hold a sheet of notebook or typing paper in each hand. Ask your audience to vote on whether blowing between the two pieces of paper will make them move apart or come closer together. Hold the papers so they are about 2 inches apart in front of your mouth. Blow hard between the papers. Your fast-flowing breath moving between the two sheets of paper will have less pressure than the surrounding air. The papers will move toward each other.

Magic in Action

About 200 years ago, Swiss scientist Daniel Bernoulli (say BER-noo-lee) discovered fast-moving air has less pressure than slow-moving air. Today, that discovery is used to help airplanes fly. The top of an airplane's wing is curved and the bottom is flat. Because air moves faster over a curved surface, there is more push from below the wing, helping lift the plane.

Encore!

The show is over so take a bow. You're not finished, though. The world is full of amazing things to investigate and the results will often seem to be magical. So keep on exploring! Once you discover the science behind what happens, you'll be ready to perform again.

Magician's Notes!

Write any notes here that might be helpful to you.